Easy Boogie-Woogie

For Beginners

Southern House Publishing

ISBN: 978-1-9997478-5-5

tylermusic.co.uk

CONTENTS

Introduction

I assume that if you are reading this then you have an interest in learning to play boogie-woogie on the piano, so I'll start by congratulating you on your fantastic taste in music. I like a fairly varied range of musical styles, but I think that boogie-woogie has to be the most enjoyable to play.

Boogie-woogie developed around the same time as the blues and was at its most popular between the 1920's and 1940's. It has a lot in common with the blues, but where blues music is more about emotion, boogie-woogie emphasized rhythm and was originally intended for dancing.

The purpose of this book is to give those that are new to boogie-woogie a first step into the style. Its aim is to cover the basics and get you started, the examples begin easy and then gradually increase in difficulty while introducing a few extra elements along the way. Once you have the basics that this book provides, you'll be at a point to then progress further with other publications of a higher difficulty level, or by using some of the sheet music that's available and hopefully from listening to the music too.

Thanks for reading this little intro, I hope you will find this book helpful on the start of your musical journey, and I further hope that you will continue on, helping to keep the music alive.

12-Bar Blues Progression

Boogie-woogie has a lot in common with the blues and this includes the form of the music. Blues commonly uses a chord progression that's twelve bars long, so boogie-woogie also tends to follows the same format. There are other chord progressions, but the twelve bar is by far the most commonly used.

The 12-bar blues progression in it's most basic form uses but three chords, which makes it quite easy to remember. Its simplicity here is frowned upon by some, but it is part of what makes the music magical in my opinion.

The three chords used in the blues are commonly referred to as being the ONE – FOUR – FIVE chords. This is more simply and commonly written as the Roman numerals I – IV – V.

You might have come across this before, but just in-case you are wondering what on earth I'm talking about, here's a brief explanation.

The 'C' Major Scale

You can see how the 'C' major scale above has had each note numbered, these are the degrees of the scale. When someone uses a Roman numeral as a chord, the number/numeral relates to the note that is numbered accordingly. So in this example the 'I' refers to the 'C' and the 'IV' refers to the 'F'.

1. equals the 'C' chord
2. equals the 'D' chord
3. equals the 'E' chord
4. equals the 'F' chord
5. equals the 'G' chord
6. equals the 'A' chord
7. equals the 'B' chord

The beauty of this system of Roman numerals is that it makes it easy to change the progression into another key, as the designation of 'II' or 'V' is not fixed to any particular chord, it's relative to the key you are playing in.

Here is an example of a basic twelve bar blues progression shown as Roman numerals. Eventually you will get used to thinking about it in these terms.

A Typical 12-Bar Blues Progression

It consists of...

- 'I'   Four bars
- 'IV'   Two bars
- 'I'   Two bars
- 'V'   One bar
- 'IV'   One bar
- 'I'   Two bars

Now with that all said and out of the way, if it's new and confusing don't worry too much about it, as we will from now on be referring to the chords used by their actual names, but at least you now hopefully get the idea, which will help you understand things in the future.

For the purpose of this book we will be keeping things in the key of 'C'. With this being a beginners guide it makes sense to keep to this for the sake of simplicity. So with that in mind, here is a twelve bar progression in the key of 'C'.

The I – IV – V chords in the key of 'C' are C – F – G. Below is the same 12-bar chord progression as before, but this time it is shown in the key of 'C'.

I   equals   the 'C' chord
IV   equals   the 'F' chord
V   equals   the 'G' chord

A Typical 12-Bar Blues Progression

Initially at least that's all there is to it, not too hard to remember, although the trick to such styles of playing is that these have to become completely internalized and recalled/used without thought, but that comes with practice.

Although it is only twelve bars long and has but three chords, it still might help you to remember the chord progression by breaking it down into three smaller sections of four bars. Not only because smaller chunks are always easier, but also because the feel of the music does kind of have three separate acts to it within its twelve bars, in a sense at least.

1.

The first four bars are all the 'C' chord. In a sense they set the scene, in blues music a little like its asking a question, in boogie-woogie it introduces the rhythmic pattern.

2.

The second four bars are 'F' and 'C' in equal measure. The 'F' is a little like an initial response to the first four bars question and often repeats the same right-hand pattern, although it's often altered to suit the new chord.

3.

The third four bars are different, the 'G' and the 'F' kind of resolve the question, with the last two bars of 'C' then setting things up for the next twelve bars. The right-hand on these bars is normally different to the pattern you began with to some extent.

Starting Out

Perhaps the most important aspect of boogie-woogie piano is the left-hand. It is a very rhythmic style of music, so it's important to develop a left-hand that can give a strong but consistent bass-line. You can fly all over the keyboard with the right-hand but if the left-hand isn't tight and strong then the music will suffer. All the best players have a strong left-hand and so it is here that we will begin.

The left-hand of boogie-woogie consists of a repeating pattern that is most often one bar long, although occasionally it can be two bars. This pattern is then repeated throughout the twelve bars and changes to match the chords. This might sound simple and technically it is, but to keep this pattern pounding out bar after bar with good timing takes practice.

There are so many different left-hand patterns to be found in boogie-woogie piano that it isn't possible to cover them all here, or in truth even scratch the surface, but we will look at perhaps the most common or popular one to begin with.

Often referred to as a kind of 'chopping bass' or even 'the chop', this can be found everywhere and is arguably the best place to start. Bare in mind that this is a proper boogie-woogie left-hand rather than something overly simplistic that isn't authentic, although initially it will be introduced in stages with the patterns in left-hand 1 and 2 being there merely to ease you into it, the pattern in left-hand 3 is the real deal.

Left-Hand 1

The left-hand pattern below is played on each individual beat. At the bottom is 'C' which is the root note of the 'C' chord we are in, this repeats on each and every beat. The other notes alternate between the fifth and the sixth, which for the 'C' chord used below is the 'G' and 'A'.

Simplified Chopping Bass

Practice this over the twelve bar blues chord progression until you feel comfortable with it. The pattern changes to match each individual chord, always with the root of the chord at the bottom as this more strongly identifies the chord.

12 Bar Chord Progression

1 🔊 AUDIO

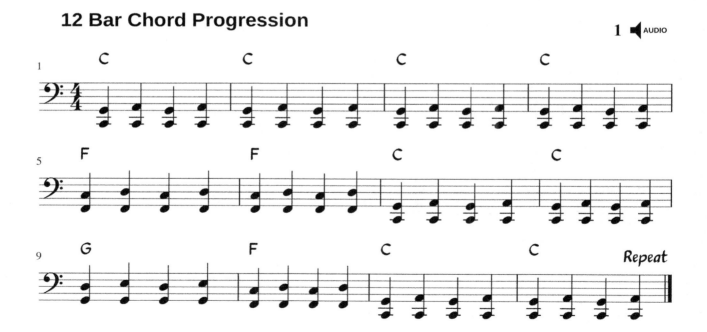

Left-Hand 2

Moving on, we now take the same pattern as before but we double up and play each note twice, switching to semi-quavers or half beats for each of the notes.

Chopping Bass-Line

Practice this over the twelve bar chord progression until you feel comfortable with it. Start at whatever tempo you require and work your way up to around 120 bpm approx.

12 Bar Chord Progression

Left-Hand 3

Once you are happy with the left-hand in example two, it's time to introduce the shuffle feel or triplet feel to the music. Boogie-woogie is rarely played straight, it is more often than not played with what is sometimes called a shuffle feel, which is another name for being played using triplet timing.

A triplet is where each beat is divided equally by three. Shown below is a bar of triplets, note how each beat (there are four with the timing being in 4/4) is divided into three notes.

When considering the timing of these, it might help to think of each individual cluster of triplets having the ¾ timing of a waltz. As such you would count three beats, 1 – 2 – 3. But instead of this count of three taking up the entire bar (as in ¾ timing) it is within the space of one beat instead.

3+4 ◀ AUDIO

You can see how each beat in the bar shares the same space as each group of triplets. Practice the timing using the count of 1 – 2 – 3 for the right-hand as you play the single bass notes.

Once you are happy with the idea of the triplets, it's time to play the 'chopping' bass as it's meant to be played.

Chopping Bass-line

Each beat is now divided into triplets, but you can see that they are not played equally. The pattern is actually split into longer notes and shorter notes, it's this constant switching between long-short, long-short that gives it the shuffle feel that you are looking for.

The first note (long note) has the count of two triplets and the second note (short) has the count of one triplet.

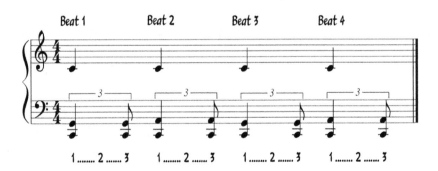

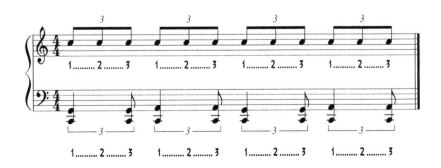

11

Chopping Bass-Line

Try this left-hand pattern over a twelve bar progression, practicing it by repeating it over and over again. If you are unsure of the sound/feel this should have then listen to the audio example or some boogie-woogie albums. Listening to the music is extremely important to help get you used to the sound and feel of boogie-woogie, the more you listen to it the more ingrained it will be become on your mind, making it easier to then re-create on the piano.

Start at whatever speed you feel comfortable and then gradually increase it as you can, up to around 120 bpm or faster if you wish. The tempo of songs that use this will naturally vary. It's important not to rush this though, as you don't want to risk losing the timing and feel for the sake of speed.

Left And Right Hands

Time to put the left-hand together with a simple right-hand. Nothing complicated, this is just using block chords so you can get used to playing with both hands together. Repeat this over and over until you are comfortable with it.

6 AUDIO

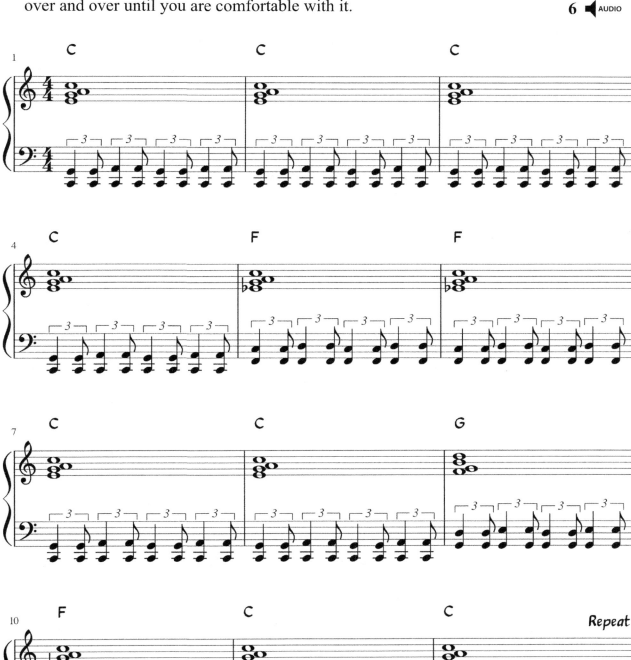

Boogie Notation Style 1

In the previous example we looked at the 'chopping' type bass-line, that like most boogie-woogie music is played with a triplet feel. This was notated using actual triplets to show you the proper timing of what you need to play, but in reality this music is never notated that way. I could continue to write the triplet feel in full triplet form, but this will only hurt you in the long run as the sheet music that you will encounter in the future won't be notated like this, so it's time to quickly cover how the triplet feel is actually conveyed in reality.

There are two different ways that you might find boogie-woogie written, one seems to be becoming far more popular these days than the other (probably due to the ease of use) but we will cover both so that you know everything.

The first currently less popular uses a method of dotted-quavers and semi-quavers. This come close to the true timing and does a nice job of implying the timing, but would sound odd if played exactly as it is.

Instead of this...

We have this...

Technically not correct, but close and does a fair job of implying the actual timing you want.

The dotted quaver takes the place of the double triplet with a count of two triplets and the semi-quaver takes the place of the single triplet with a count of one triplet.

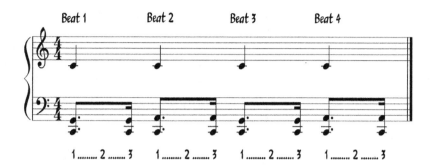

This is easy enough when you know that it's actually in triplet time, which listening to boogie-woogie will naturally have you doing anyway. As said, this method doesn't seem quite so prevalent anymore, but when you do come across this in a boogie-woogie transcription then you will understand how it is played.

Have a quick play of the left-hand while reading the quaver/semi-quaver notation just to get used to the idea. Remember that it is played the same as the previous version written as triplets.

Notation Style 1

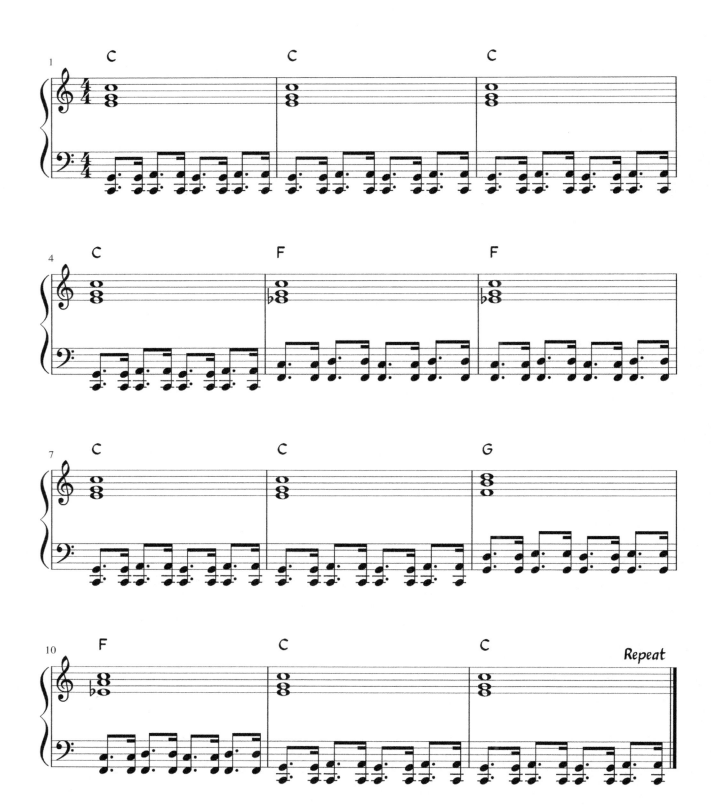

Boogie Notation Style 2

The next method of notating boogie-woogie music seems to becoming the more accepted and common method, which is probably due to the ease and speed at which it can be written. This is a simpler way that just uses quavers throughout.

Triplet Feel Bass As Quavers

You have probably noticed that this looks exactly the same as the left-hand pattern shown on page nine, and you'd be right. But although it is written the same way, it isn't actually played as strict quavers.

Looking at the example below, the first quaver of the bass-line represents the double triplet and has a count of two triplets. The second quaver represents the single triplet note and has a count of one triplet.

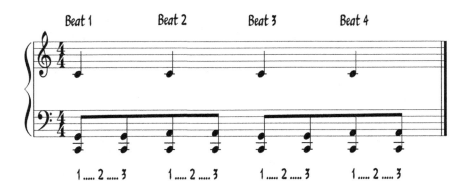

Instead of this...

We have this...

This is obviously not technically correct in the slightest but all the notes are there, so as long as you know that the piece is to be played with a triplet feel then all is good with the world. Naturally you need some way of knowing that a piece of sheet music is in a triplet feel, so you will see a sign at the beginning of a piece that informs you of the fact.

Typical Sign Denoting Triplet Feel

I know having different ways of writing the same thing may seem confusing or at least a little strange, but now that you are aware of this you won't be confused by the sheet music available, and it will most likely be written in this manner, so this is a very important point to get used to early on.

Bare in mind that there is an exception to this quaver only method, and that is when all three notes in a group of triplets are sounded out. Then of course the notation reverts back to using the proper full triplet notation.

Have a quick play of the left-hand while reading the quaver only notation just to get used to the idea. Remember that it is played the same as the first version written in triplets.

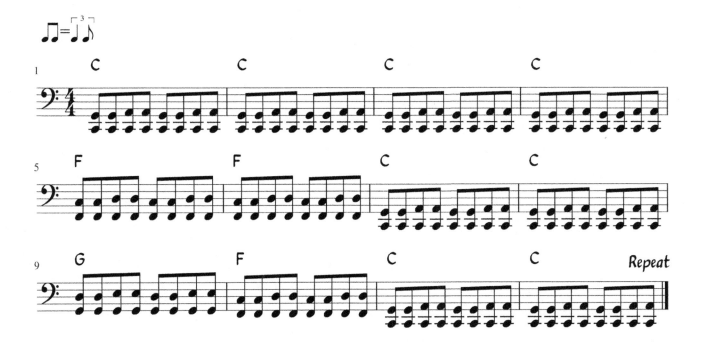

Notation Style 2

Chord Comping 1

Before we look at any boogie-woogie style riffs with the right-hand, we shall have a quick look at using chords in a rhythmic fashion to comp over the left-hand. We will have a look at two common patterns that you will find used a lot in many songs.

Here is the first pattern that we are taking a look at. The chord is played on the first beat and just before the fourth beat.

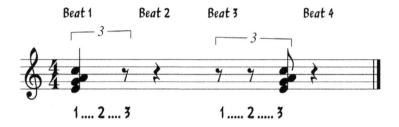

The first chord is worth the count of two triplets with the second chord being worth the count of one triplet. But the second chord is played on the last count in the triplet group of beat three. This is easier to understand when looked at with the left-hand, as you can see exactly where the chord-lands in relation to the bass-line.

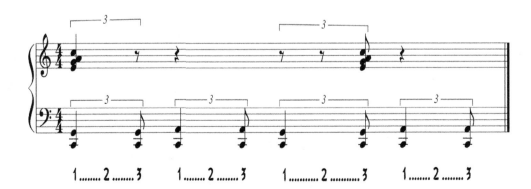

Chord Comp 1

22

Chord Comp 1 continued...

Chord Comping 2

The next example uses a different rhythmic pattern. The first chord now lands on the last triplet of beat one and the second chord on the first triplet of beat three.

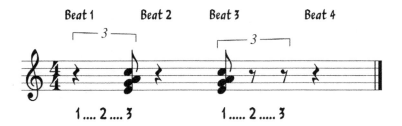

In Relation To The Left-Hand

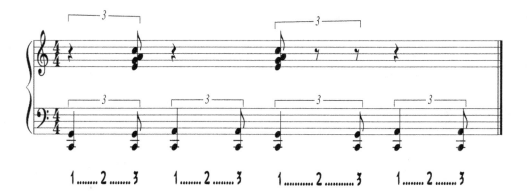

Chord Comp 2

Chord Comp 2 continued...

Right-Hand Melody

Beyond using just chords in a rhythmic fashion, boogie-woogie is obviously also melodic so we shall begin looking at what you might play with the right-hand.

Although all styles of music vary, they tend to have a standard form to which they adhere to. Boogie-woogie tends to be created by a series of rhythmic or melodic patterns. In a typical boogie-woogie a particular pattern is played over the twelve bar progression, changing slightly to suit each specific chord.

A simple pattern using thirds on the 'I' chord.

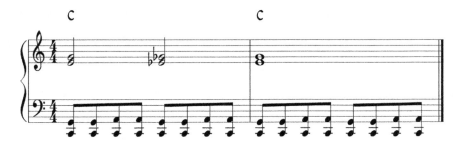

When changing to the 'IV' chord the same pattern is carried over, but here it has changed key to match the different chord.

Have a look at 'First Boogie-Woogie' and get used to this idea of patterns within the songs.

First Boogie-Woogie

First Boogie-Woogie continued...

Second 12 Bars

Right-Hand Melody

The next example piece is very similar, but starts to add triplet timing to the right-hand as well as the left. The nice thing about this is that you will find that a lot of the time the notes of the right and left hands coincide, landing together at the same time. This is part of the feel of the music, but does make it easier when starting out.

The right-hand pattern here uses a triplet feel on the last beat. The 'D' and 'F' are for the count of two triplets, with the E♭ and G♭ having the count of one triplet. You can see how this lines up directly with the triplet feel left-hand, making it easier to play the two together.

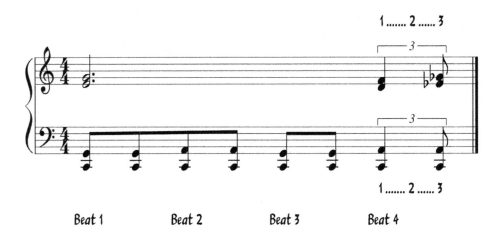

Beat 1   Beat 2   Beat 3   Beat 4

Practice the next two example pieces 'Thirds Boogie-Woogie' and 'Another Boogie' until you are comfortable with them. These will help get you used to playing the triplet feel with both hands at the same time.

Thirds Boogie-Woogie

First 12 Bars

31

Thirds Boogie-Woogie continued...

Another Boogie

Another Boogie continued...

Second 12 Bars

Left-Hand 4

This left-hand bass-line is quite similar to the 'chopping' style of bass-line we have already covered, but has it's own distinct character.

Compared to the 'chopping' bass, the second half of beat two and four have been changed, now using the third as a single note, for the 'C' chord that is the note 'E'.

Practice the left-hand individually over a twelve bar progression until you feel comfortable with it. This helps with left/right hand independence.

35

Breakfast Boogie

Breakfast Boogie continued...

Pete's Boogie

Pete's Boogie continued...

Boogie-Woogie Lane

Boogie-Woogie Lane continued...

Second 12 Bars

Left-Hand 5

This left-hand pattern uses the same notes as the basic 'chopping' type bass-line, but now they are being played separately on an alternate basis.

The long and short timing of the triplet feel remains the same.

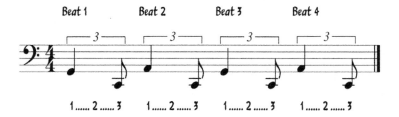

Practice the left-hand separately to start with until you are comfortable with it. Note that on each chord change the first note of the new chord is played as the last note of the previous bar and chord. Although optional, this helps makes the transition between chords easier and smoother.

42

Lunch-Time Boogie

Lunch-Time Boogie continued...

Left-Hand 6

The left-hand pattern shown here is again based around the same format as the 'chopping' type bass we started with, but here the second and third beats are altered with the minor third and third being brought into use.

The long and short timing of the triplet feel remains the same.

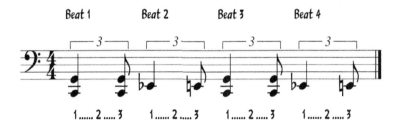

Practice the left-hand separately to start with until you are comfortable with playing it.

Boogie Street

First 12 Bars

46

Boogie Street continued...

Triplets In Boogie

So far we have looked at the use of triplets to create the triplet feel in the music, but this requires them to be used in a long/short manner as opposed to being groups of three notes.

Boogie-woogie also uses triplets in their full state, being three single notes divided equally over a single beat. This can be seen mixed into the music or for longer passages of repeating patterns of only triplets.

Practice this kind of thing individually at first before adding the left-hand. It may look busy and therefore complicated, but in reality it is just three notes at a time repeating over and over. As always, start off slowly and gradually increase the tempo as you can.

Triple The Boogie

Triple The Boogie continued...

Second 12 Bars

Walking Bass

A walking bass-line can be found in many styles of music and this includes boogie-woogie. This isn't perhaps the easiest type of left-hand used in boogie-woogie, but it is maybe the most fun.

The walking-bass gets its name from the way that it walks up and down the scale/keyboard. There are so many ways and variations of doing this and it can be as complicated or as simple as you wish to make it, but for now we start off simple.

This example uses single notes, each one beat long. It begins on the root of the chord, moves up through the 3rd, 5th and 6th, before hitting the root an octave higher and moving back down again.

Practice the bass-line on its own to begin with, the timing is simple but there is a fair amount of movement over the keyboard.

22 AUDIO

51

Slow Walk Boogie

Slow Walk Boogie continued...

Octave Walking Bass

The walking-bass is most commonly played in boogie-woogie as octaves. The pattern is the same as already covered, it's just that now all notes are now half beats and each one is played once and then a second time an octave higher. This makes for a great up and down motion to the left-hand and is much more exciting to listen to.

This is of course much harder to play than the single notes. Being half-beats the note frequency has doubled and the alternating motion between the octave notes is difficult, and those with smaller hands might struggle with the octave stretch. It all depends on your current level of playing, but try it out, it's good fun and with practice eventually it will come to you.

Walk The Boogie

Walk The Boogie continued...

Walk The Boogie continued...

Last Time Boogie

To finish with we have a slightly longer boogie-woogie piece that combines some of the examples used in the book together to create a short boogie-woogie kind of song.

This example shows how each of the twelve bar sections tend to vary, with a different pattern or a variation of an existing pattern that has already been used.

I've opted to use the basic 'chopping' style left-hand for this, but feel free to change this to any of the others if you feel you can and want to, or even vary them throughout.

The tempo is entirely up to you and where you feel comfortable playing. I'd suggest working up to anything between 120 bpm to 160 bpm, but as in all music, start off slower and gradually increase the pace as and when possible.

Last Time Boogie

Last Time Boogie continued...

Last Time Boogie continued...

3rd 12 Bars

61

Last Time Boogie continued...

4th 12 Bars

Last Time Boogie continued...

5th 12 Bars

Last Time Boogie continued...

6th 12 Bars

Practice Suggestions

Practice Time

I will state the obvious and say that to progress and improve at anything you need to spend time doing that thing. So needless to say that the more time you spend on the piano the better you will get. But I will say one thing, consistency is the key. The best way to progress is to practice everyday, this keeps everything fresh in your mind and will really help push you forward. And when I say everyday, it doesn't necessarily mean hours and hours (although if you can then great, the more the merrier) just put in whatever you can spare, even ten minutes if that's all you have, the main thing is to keep it regular without large gaps in-between.

Metronome

Using a metronome while practicing is highly recommended. The use of one will really help with keeping the timing tight throughout and also when learning a part that has timing you are unaccustomed to. When I say metronome, use whatever you have, which may literally be a mechanical metronome or one on an electric instrument or even an app on your phone. Playing along to a drum backing is also an option, and there are a few drum tracks available to download, although these are of course at set tempos.

Listen To The Music

To really get the feel of boogie-woogie it is vital that you listen to it as much as possible. This really helps you internalize the sound, which in turn will help enable you to recreate it on the piano. There is a short list of possible starting points on the suggested listening page, just in-case you're not sure where to start.

Suggested Listening

Without doubt one of the most important things you can do when learning a style of music is to listen to it, and I mean a lot. This may sound obvious, but you really want to make a point of listening to the music that you are trying to play. While you can learn songs merely from reading sheet music, the dots and dashes really don't convey the feeling of the music the same way and the brain absorbs the sounds that you hear which makes it far easier to then translate that sound onto the piano.

The listed albums are only suggestions to help get you started and are all from my own collection. Some of these albums date back to the time of the original masters with some being compilations of the old classics (as albums at the time were relatively rare). Other albums here are from more recent exponents of the genre, as fortunately there are still new pianists appearing and hopefully will continue to do so.

Take note, that there are many boogie-woogie compilations out there for sale today, while there's nothing wrong with these, just be careful not to buy too many and end up having many duplicates of the same songs.

Suggested Listening

Albert Ammons & Pete Johnson: 8 To The Bar

Albert Ammons/Johnson/Meade Lux Lewis:
The boogie Woogie Trio Vols 1 – 2

Albert Ammons: Boogie Woogie King

Meade Lux Lewis/Ammons/Johnson/Yancy:
Masters Of Boogie Woogie/Five Album Set

Jimmy Yancey/Ammons/Johnson:
Boogie Woogie Man

Axel Zwingenberger: Live

Axel Zwingenberger: Boogie Woogie Classics

Axel Zwingenberger:
Boogie Woogie Breakdown

Jools Holland: Solo Piano

Silvan Zingg: Boogie Woogie Triology

Silvan Zingg: Boogie Woogie Ride

Vince Weber: The Boogie Man

Chris Conz Trio: Drivin' The Boogie

Luca Sestak: New Way

Henri Herbert: Boogie Woogie Piano

Various Artists (Many / 10 Cd Box Set):
200 Legendary Boogie Woogie Hits

Downloadable Audio

Audio files based on the examples within the book
are available to download from the website in MP3
format, simply follow the instructions below.

To access and download the MP3 audio files,
simply visit the website...

www.tylermusic.co.uk

- Click on audio downloads
- Select the relevant book title
- Enter the password... **easywoogie855**
- Click on download icon

Once downloaded please save them for future use.

Downloadable Audio Files

1) Bass Left-Hand 1
2) Bass Left-Hand 2
3) Triplet Timing Slow
4) Triplet Timing Fast
5) Bass Left-Hand 3
6) Left And Right Hands
7) Chord Comp 1
8) Chord Comp 2
9) First Boogie-Woogie
10) Third Boogie-Woogie
11) Another Boogie
12) Bass Left-Hand 4
13) Breakfast Boogie
14) Pete's Boogie
15) Boogie-Woogie Lane
16) Bass Left-Hand 5
17) Lunch-Time Boogie
18) Bass Left-Hand 6
19) Boogie Street
20) R/H Triplet Patterns
21) Triple The Boogie
22) Walking Bass Single
23) Slow Walk Boogie
24) Walking Bass Octaves
25) Walk The Boogie
26) Last Time Boogie
27) Drum Track 100 bpm
28) Drum Track 120 bpm

Take The Next Step...

If you're enjoying learning boogie-woogie piano then this series of books will be perfect for you.

Improvising Boogie-Woogie

The best next step from Easy Boogie-Woogie is this series of three books designed to take your boogie-woogie piano to the next level.

Improvising Boogie-Woogie
Volumes Two And Three

**The boogie-woogie piano series of three volumes that combine to a
massive 450 pages (approx) of some of the best
boogie-woogie education available today.**

**Each volume covers different aspects of playing, taking a detailed look at
different left-hand patterns and various techniques you can employ with
the right-hand. Song examples are included to help practice everything.
Complete with downloadable audio.**

A few samples of content subjects...

- **Left-hand patterns**
- **Right-hand riffs**
- **Right-hand comping**
- **Right-hand techniques**
- **How to use scales**
- **Creating your own riffs**
- **New chord progression**
- **Playing in different keys**
- **Rhythmic ideas**
- **Introducing stride**
- **Using thirds and sixths**
- **And much more. . .**

Also Available

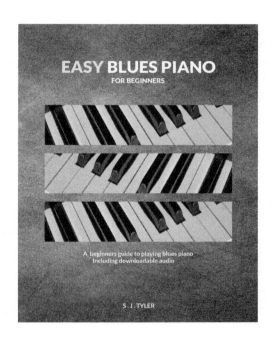

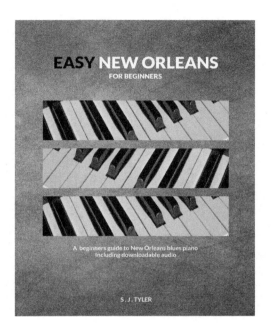

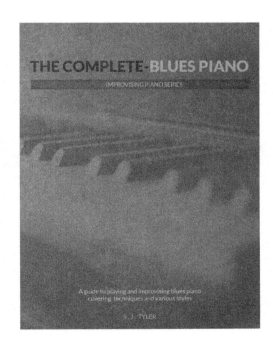

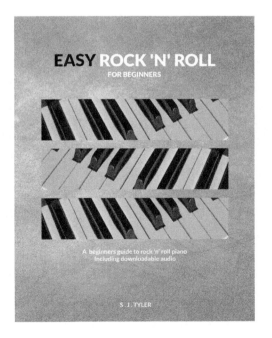

Tyler music.co.uk

For further piano books, sheet music and information on blues
and boogie woogie music and events
visit the website at...

www.tylermusic.co.uk

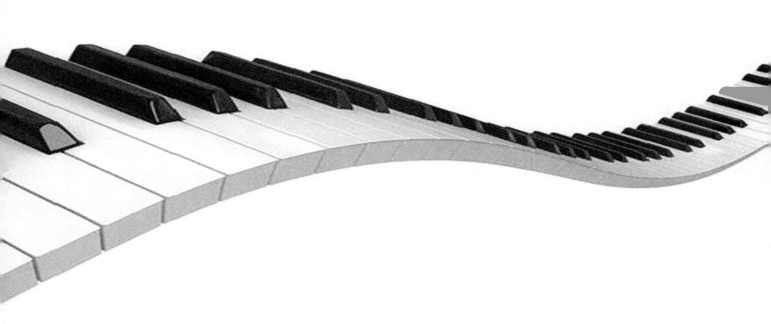

Printed in Great Britain
by Amazon